THE

STATE SOVEREIGNTY RECORD OF MASSACHUSETTS.

BY

A SON OF NORFOLK.

NORFOLK, VA:
J. W. FATHERLY, BOOK AND JOB PRINTER, 157 MAIN ST
1872.

PREFATORY.

RICHMOND, VA., November 15, 1872.

S. S. Dawes, Esq.,

Norfolk, Va.,

DEAR SIR:—You doubtless recollect the conversation I held with you a short time ago, in which I casually mentioned to you some of the evidences I had gathered of the diametrically opposite positions which the State of Massachusetts has held on the subject of State Sovereignty in two distinct periods of her history; and that you then suggested to me the expediency of putting these evidences together in some durable form for the information of the reading public of the South, and peradventure of some of the Northern people.

Reflecting on what you said, I at last decided to act on your suggestion, and, accordingly in the form of a letter to yourself, have thrown together, in the following pages, some important and ineffaceable facts in the political record of Massachusetts, which I have here and there interspersed with a few comments and reflections of my own naturally suggested by those facts.

That I should publicly address the following pages to yourself I consider especially appropriate, because it was from your own suggestion the work has been written, and because of your well known consistent and unchangeable devotion to the political truths for which our Revolutionary forefathers successfully contended, and who little thought that those truths and the system of government they adopted, were to be ruthlessly overthrown and scornfully trampled under foot ere the lapse of one short century after their vast sacrifices and Herculean efforts in the cause of free government.

With sentiments of the highest esteem, I am,

Dear Sir, very truly, your friend,

A SON OF NORFOLK.

Table of Errata, Omissions and Insertions.

Page 3, line 12.—Insert "the" before "freedom."

Page 5, line 35.—Change "a" into "e" in the word "independant."

Page 6, line 13.—Change "1775" into "1793."

Page 10, line 4.—Insert "t" in the word "Harford."

Page 11, line 31.—Insert "as above described" after the word "confederacy."

Page 11, line 37.—Change the first "as" into "so."

Page 16, line 23.—Strike out the word "for."

Page 20, line 24.—Change "McBeth" into "MacBeth."

Page 20, line 31.—Insert "the" before "above."

Page 23, line 2.—Insert "of other" after the word "record."

Page 23, line 7.—Transpose the letters "i e" in the word "soveriegnty."

Page 24, line 1.—Insert "of 1789" after the word "confederacy."

THE STATE--SOVEREIGNTY
RECORD OF MASSACHUSETTS.

———o———

RICHMOND, VA:—November 13, 1872.

S. S. Dawes, Esq.,
Norfolk, Va.,

DEAR SIR:—I have noticed in a recent number of the *Boston Advertiser*, (a Republican Journal,) some editorial comments on the results of the late Presidential election; and among those comments I was particularly struck by this remark of the editor, (as if he were announcing an event of great public benefit,) viz:

"STATE SOVEREIGNTY IS DEAD."

What a melancholy, deplorable fact, what a commentary on the rapid political degeneracy of the American people in the short space of ninety-six years it is, that, in any quarter of the Union, an exponent of the opinions of the dominating and most numerous party can now be found exulting in so awful a public misfortune as the destruction of the means and support of freedom of local government, the great right for which among others, the fathers successfully fought, and established with the most jealous care on, as they thought, the firmest of foundations.

But if State Sovereignty is dead, *who killed it?* Surely not the people of the South; for they, as the whole world knows, fought to sustain it. If it was one of the most prominent features of the compact between the States, the very corner stone of the Constitution and Union, then they who overthrew it, if at the time living under it, were revolutionists, and therefore rebels; and the *Advertiser* thus, by its own dictum, convicts the people of the North of being the *real* rebels in the late war between the States.

Was it indeed the corner stone of the Constitution, or a myth which in reality never had any support or basis in the Constitution, as the despotic party which now rules the country, actually asserts and affects to believe? In order that objection, on the score of latitude, may not be made by our "enemies," (Boutwell *meo auctore* for this expression,) if I should introduce Southern testimony for the solution of this question, I will therefore cite *Northern* witnesses to the stand, and in fact Massachusetts only, saving one or two brief exceptions.

When the present Federal Constitution was placed, as it originally came from the hands of its framers, before the people of Massachusetts, in Convention in 1788, for acceptance or rejection by them in their own separate behalf, as they in their full, separate, and absolute sovereignty might see fit to do, they, (disapproving of it as it then stood,) yet accepted and ratified it, with the confident expectation however and a clear understanding from the friends of the Constitution, that the following (among others) important explanatory declaration, (then drawn up and proposed by Massachusetts herself,) should speedily be added to and become an Article of the Constitution; viz: (and these are her own words,) "That it be explicitly declared that all powers not expressly *delegated* by the aforesaid Constitution, are reserved to the *several* States, to be by them exercised."

Massachusettts saw, when the Constitution was first laid before her in the condition in which it had come from the hands of its framers, that if not amended in the mode indicated by her proposed declaratory article, the artful lovers of power and prerogative might and doubtless would, as time wore on, endeavor to establish, from the general tenor of the Constitution as it had come from the hands of the framers, that the people by their ratifications had *merged* their several separate State Sovereignties into, what has since proved to be that capacious reservoir of power, the General Government, and had thus voluntarily instituted and intended to institute *one* great perfectly-sovereign political community called "The People of the United States." To prevent any chance of this, Massachusetts provided for the addition to the Constitution of her "explicit" declaration, (in which she inserted the word "*delegated*" to preclude the idea even of alienation,) and, as it were, stipulated for that addition by formally appending the declaration to her own ratification of the Constitution when she sent the latter to Congress. So much opposed was a large portion of her State Convention to ratifying the Constitution *before* her proposed amendments should be added to it, that, out of three hundred and fifty five members composing it, only one hundred and eighty seven could be persuaded to vote for ratification without the addition of the amendments prior to ratification; and the larger portion of those who did vote for ratification voted thus because of assurances made to them that the Constitution should be amended without delay.

It is worth while to notice here, that, notwithstanding this wise precaution of Massachusetts, the great historian Motley has, within a few years past in a grave and important work, unblushingly stated, in the face of Article VII, of the Constitution itself, (which says: "The ratification of the conventions of nine *States* shall be sufficient for the establishment of this Constitution *between the States* so ratifying the same,") and in direct contradiction of the Tenth Amendment and of the well known and recorded facts of the case, that the people of the United States, as *one* people, one consolidated political community, ordained and established the Constitution, and vested Congress with the sovereign powers it exercises.

Thousands of otherwise well informed people at the North who have read Motley, but who have not studied the Constitution for themselves nor investigated the *facts of its history* and the concomitant political history of the several political communities concerned in framing it and putting it in operation, religiously believe his utterly unfounded dictum on this subject.

But to go back to Massachusetts' "explicit declaration." In accordance with her desire and with that of some of the other States, this declaration was, in fulfillment of the assurances that had been made, proposed by Congress, at its first session under the present Constitution, to the several States as an amendment to the Constitution, and, as soon as the necessary legal forms could be gone through for the purpose, (to-wit in 1791,) it became a declaratory Article of the Constitution now known as the Tenth Amendment or Article; and thus, as an authoritative commentary on the Constitution itself, it definitively and, as was then supposed, forever settled the question of State Sovereignty, and decided that the Government of the United States possessed no original underived, inherent sovereingty of its own, or represented any such sovereignty as existing in *one* consolidated political community, but was the mere recipient only of the right to exercise, for the benefit of *the States*, a certain few specified "powers" of sovereignty that were only "*delegated*" (*not* alienated) to it by the several really sovereign parties to the compact, viz: the States, who each separately and for itself looked to no Constitution whatever (State or Federal) and to no earthly power outside of itself for the warrant of its own inherent and underived, independant sovereignty.

This was the first step, so far as the present Constitution of the United States is concerned, that Massachusetts took to assert the existence of and to provide a Constitutional guarantee for the security of State Sovereignty; and notwithstanding her recreancy in recent years and at present from her earlier grand and prominent position in these matters, she yet will deserve the gratitude of posterity, (should

State Sovereignty be ever again recovered,) for her noble and successful stand in this behalf in the earlier days of the Republic.

Massachusetts again stood forth the vindicator of State Sovereignty, when by the mouth of Judge Sullivan, her Attorney General, and afterwards Judge of the Supreme Court and Governor of the State, she said, (in 1791,) of the present Federal Constitution, that it was "a *compact* between the *States*," being a repitition of her more solemn and authoritative declaration of 1788, recorded in her act of ratification of the Constitution, where she terms it "an *explicit* compact "as if intending to indicate by the use of the word "explicit" that it was expressed too plainly to be susceptible of more than one interpretation.

A third time did Massachusetts put in an appearance in energetic and successful defence of State Sovereignty, when in 1775, her Governor, John Hancock, and her Attorney General, James Sullivan, were summoned by the U. S. Marshall to appear in court and, as the representatives of the sovereignty of Massachusetts, to answer to a suit of a citizen of another State. The Governor *refused to obey the summons*, although the Constitution provided for just such cases, and authorized this citizen to sue Massachusetts. The Governor forthwith summoned a meeting of the Legislature; and in his opening speech to them he said, "I cannot conceive that the people of this Commonwealth, who by their representatives adopted the Federal *compact*, expected a State would be held liable to answer a cumpulsory civil process to an individual of another State or foreign kingdom." He also said that a "consolidation of the States into *one* government would endanger the nation as a Republic, and *eventually divide the States* now united, or *eradicate* the principles for which we have contended," meaning the principles fought for in the then recent Revolutionary War. Did he in prophetic mood then look forward to the present time and predict the wonders that now are being, and for the last eleven years have been enacted in this—what shall I call it? certainly not, Republic.

In view of the exigency in which the Legislature of Massachusetts thus found their State, they passed on the 27th September, 1793, the following resolution, viz:

"*Resolved*, That a power claimed of compelling the State to become a defendant at the suit ot an individual or individuals, is unnecessary and inexpedient, and in its exercise dangerous to the power, safety, and *independence* of the *several* States and repugnant to the *first principles* of a *Confederate* government."

Accordingly, to prevent the chance of any other attempt at offering such an indignity to a Sovereign State, Massachusetts again proposed a farther amendment to the Federal Constitution as an additional guard and guarantee of State Sovereignty, and it was adopted and is now known as the Eleventh Amendment. John Hancock, James Sullivan, Samuel Adams, Doctor Jarvis, Nathan Dane and many other great and leading men of Massachusetts took a very active and energetic part in this successful vindication of State Sovereignty.—[*Fowler.*]

We see here that this State was then so determined to entrench State Sovereignty in an impregnable position, that she actually proposed and procured the *annulment* of an original provision of the Constitution, viz: that provision in Section 2d, of Article III, which empowered a citizen of any State to sue any other State. And there to this day does that provision stand in the Constitution, *a dead letter*, forever void and of no effect, and utterly killed by the procurement of Massachusetts alone in her persistent efforts to guard securely and firmly establish the great controlling feature of the American system of Federal Government, State Sovereignty.

Again did Massachusetts stand up stoutly for the firm establishment of State Sovereignty, (although in this instance, I go backwards in my chronology of her noble persistence,) when through the voice of the great Samuel Adams, who was afterwards Lieutenant Governor of the State, she said, (in her ratifying convention of 1788,) of the declaratory amendment before referred to, that it "was consonant with the Second Article in the present (meaning the then existing first) confederation, viz: that *each* State retains its *sovereignty*, *freedom and independence*, and every power, jurisdiction and right which is not by this confederation expressly *delegated* to the United States in Congress assembled." Observe just here particularly, that Samuel Adams by claiming the Tenth Amendment of the present Constitution to be the equivalent of the Second Article of the first Constitution, plainly claims that the sovereignty itself resides in the States, not the States collectively, but separately in "*each*" State, and that certain "powers" of sovereignty, (that is to say, not the sovereignty itself but the right to exercise certain *powers* thereof,) are only "delegated," not alienated to Congress. This is just what the Tenth Amendment in the present Constitution asserts, and was intended, (on the motion of Massachusetts herself made out of abundant caution,) to declare.

When Samuel Adams was appointed Lieut. Governor, (John Hancock being Governor,) he said, referring to his induction into office, "I shall be called upon to make a declaration, and I shall do it cheerfully, that the Commonwealth of Massachusetts is and *of right* ought to be a free *sovereign* and independent State. I shall be called upon to make another declaration with the same solemnity, (his oath,) *to support the Constitution of the United States.* I see no inconsistency in this." Nor needed he to have seen it; for, while Massachusetts should choose to remain in the Confederacy, she herself, and therefore her State officers, would be in law and in honour bound to observe the terms of the compact. But there would have been very great inconsistency in his making these two declarations at the same time, if the "United *States* in Congress Assembled" were not the mere governmental agency of a Confederacy, but were the representatives of *one* consolidated political community having original, inherent sovereignty of its own. Thus in these utterances of Samuel Adams, did Massachusetts for the fifth time declare State Sovereignty to be the corner stone of her political creed.

For the sixth time did this State declare her belief in State Sovereignty on the occasion of the Embargo, (declared in December 1807,) when it was well understood that not very long after the declaration, she intended *forcible resistance* and *secession* if it should not be speedily repealed. When the Embargo was laid, it so enraged the people of Massachusetts and of other New England States that a convention of delegates from those States to meet in New Haven was proposed and intended.–[*Fowler.*] John Quincy Adams writing to Mr. Giles, of Virginia, on this subject urged that "a continuation of the Embargo much longer would *certainly* be met by *forcible resistance* supported by the Legislature (of Mass.,) and probably by the judiciary of the State." And he added to the foregoing thus: "That the object of the leaders had been, for several years, *the dissolution of the Union*, and the establishment of a *separate Confederation*, I know from *unequivocal evidence.*" [*See Niles' Register*, Vol. XXXV, p. 138.] Here we have Massachusetts giving to South Carolina at an early day emphatic lessons in the art of threatening, and, under certain contingencies, in the purpose of performing not only nullification but secession.

In consequence of this apprehended forcible resistance and, if not actual, yet threatened secession of New England, led on by Massachusetts, the Embargo was repealed on 1st March, 1809, just before the retirement of Mr. Jefferson from the Presidential office.

For the seventh time did Massachusetts, true to her early State-Rights record, assert the independent sovereignty of the States and the merely confederative character of the Union, when in 1810, in reply to a communication from the Governor, her Legislature said: "The *allegiance* they owe to the Commonwealth as a *Sovereign*, *Independent* State," &c., and in the same reply added, "this Commonwealth forms an important member of the National *Confederacy*."

In 1812 we find this State for the eighth time standing up stoutly and defiantly towards the General Government in vindication of her independent sovereignty. On the 18th of June, 1812, war was declared by the United States against Great Britain almost solely in the interest of Massachusetts and other New England States. When, soon after this declaration, a requisition was made by the General Government, in pursuance of authority given by the Constitution, on Governor Strong, of Massachusetts, for forty-one companies of infantry and artillery, he, taking the position that he was the representative of an Independent Sovereignty, endued with the right of judging of the righfulness of the requisition, *positively refused* to furnish the troops called for. He officially communicated this refusal to the Legislature of his State, and that body as well as the people of the State approved his course. [*See Mass. Reports*, Vol. VIII, p. 548.]

In the war of 1812–15, we find this State for the ninth time standing out in the bold assertion of her sovereignty, and doing this too by an overt act. During the progress of the war, [*Fowler*] her Legislature passed a law directing the jailers of the State jails "to discharge at the end of thirty days all British officers captured in the war, and who had been committed to their custody for close confinement," if not removed before the end of the thirty days. If the people of Massachusetts were not a distinct independent sovereignty, holding that sovereignty as older than, and not deriving its existence from the Federal Constitution, nor from the fiat of any sovereignty or power outside of themselves, but on the contrary were only a mere fraction of one great political community of original and inherent sovereignty, viz: the so-called "People of the United States," then, beyond all, peradventure, this legislative act was, according to the position taken in the late war by Massachusetts herself, not the act of any legislature whatever, but the unauthorized proceedings of a combination of insurrectionary individuals; and those persons who pretended to be the State Legislature, and all persons supporting them in this matter were traitors and amenable to all the pains and penalties of treason against the United States for "adhereing to their enemies and giving them aid and comfort."

In the remonstrance of the Legislature of Massachusetts to Congress, of 14th June, 1813, this State for the tenth time adhered to her State Sovereignty doctrine, when she says in that remonstrance, "If any extensive *Confederate* Republic is to be maintained, and we fervently pray it may, it can only be by a free communication of the grievances felt," &c., and so on, to the end of the remonstrance.

The eleventh instance of this State's consistent faithfulness to the doctrine of State Sovereignty occurred in December, 1814. In that month and year the New England States, with Massachusetts as their leader, met in Convention in Harford, Connecticut, with what has been always well known, the intention of preparing for secession from the Union under certain contingencies. After deliberations running through the space of three weeks, the Convention made a report, which the Legislature of Massachusetts approved of by a strong vote, and appointed a committee to report on the doings of the Convention. This Committee reported as follows: "The Committee entertain a high sense of the wisdom and ability with which this Convention have discharged their arduous duty, and while they maintain the principle of *State Sovereignty*, and of the duties which citizens owe to their respective State governments," &c. In this report they term the Federal Constitution a "*compact.*" The House adopted this report by a vote of one hundred and fifty-nine ayes to only forty-eight dissentients, thus showing in a most marked manner in what light Massachusetts at that day regarded State Sovereignty.

For the twelfth time we find Massachusetts, in 1827, through the voice of one of her most distinguished, and, within her borders, most popular sons, (to-wit, John Quincy Adams, then at the head of the General Government,) proclaiming that if a State *does* indeed transgress beyond its powers as reserved to it in the Federal Constitution, it yet is not thereby divested of its State-hood, but is still a sovereign.

President Adams in his special message of February 5th, 1827, relative to the resistance of Georgia to Federal requisitions said, when adverting to civil officers of that State, acting under the orders of their State, as follows: "The surveyors are therefore not to be viewed in the light of individual and solitary transgressors, but as the agents of a *Sovereign* State acting in obedience to authority which they believed to be binding on them." If this be so, how then could the State of Massachusetts and the United States Government with any show of justice or the slightest foundation in right, believe or affect to believe that the citizens of the Confederate States in the late war were guilty of treason against the United States as a mere combination of insurrectionary individuals acting without authority from any sovereign power?

They, Massachusetts and the United States Government, affected to believe, that, because certain Sovereign States did in their acts of secession do wrong, therefore the wrongful acts of such states were, *ab initio*, void, unauthoritative and of no effect, and that the State Sovereignties attempting such acts therefore and thereby *ceased to exist;* as if, (God save the mark!) a *Sovereign* power, whenever it does wrong, thereby ceases to be a sovereign and utterly dies! The dolts! (or rather the hypocrites, for they *knew better*,) did they not know that in every war, waged wherever and whenever on the face of the earth, one of the parties to it must be, *ex necessitate rei*, always in the wrong? Do they not know that, according to their baseless and shameless assumptions, (the Massachusetts of the first half of this century herself being the judge,) if France should next week declare and wage war against Great Britain, and Great Britain should think France to be in the wrong in so doing, then Great Britain, if successful in the war, would be justified in punishing every captured French soldier or citizen taken in the act of aiding his country, as a member of a mere mob of insurrectionary persons acting only on their own individual responsibility?

Methinks I hear some Massachusetts devotee of usurping and despotic power respond that States united under one General Government stand in vastly different relations to each other as to war between themselves, from the relations, as to this particular, existing between Great Britain and France not associated in such a Union. The prompt and sufficient reply to this response, and one that will utterly pulverize it and strew its dust upon the winds, lies in the correct answer to the following two questions, viz:

First, are the associated States united in a "Confederacy" by a mutual "compact" between themselves as equals, and "delegating" only, (*not* alienating) certain, few, specified, limited "powers" to the General Government?

And Second, is the separate, distinct sovereignty which each State claims for itself an original, inherent sovereignty underived from, not conferred by, and not depending for its existence on the compact? If the answer, as applicable to any confederacy anywhere or at any time on the face of the earth, be in the affirmative, (and the record of Massachusetts, as here presented for sixty years after her accession to the Union, steadily gives such answer as to the American Union,) then to the supposed Massachusetts devotee of power and usurpation, common sense and the established maxims of Public Law would say, there is not and there could not be the slightest difference (as far as the waging of war is concerned,) in the two cases; for war in every age has been held by all publicists and all governments to rupture, abrogate and *abolish all compacts* between sovereign powers, and to remit the original parties thereto to the *original status and relations* which they held towards each other *ante fœdus.*

Although doubtless the unscrupulous party now dominating this country would unblushingly reply to the foregoing by saying, (and of course without the slightest foundation in truth,) that there was *no* compact between the States when the present Union was formed, yet the political record of the Massachusetts of the first sixty years of that Union, utterly precludes *her* from opening her mouth on the subject, except to say that there *was* a compact between the States.

A moiety of the people of Spain, in her civil troubles commencing about three years ago, intended, (and they came very near to success,) to establish a system of confederated states composed of the present provinces of the country and embracing all her territory, each state to have its own state government and control of its own local affairs. But in doing this did the people of Spain intend at the same time to abolish, to proclaim as forever dead and departed, their own national, original and inherent *one* supreme sovereignty which has existed over all Spain, whether held by kings or otherwise, as *one*, indivisible thing for many centuries? Did they intend that at the moment the confederacy should be formed, this sovereignty should die, and that the one sovereign people of Spain should then as a political community die also, and that succeeding to it, by their consent, should arise over the territory of *each* of the several new states a separate, perfect, independent and thus original State Sovereignty acknowledging no other existing sovereignty as the source and measure of its own power? By no manner of means. The Spanish people were and are not such simpletons. They, like all possessors of sovereignty, whether obtained by usurpation, (as is the case now in this country,) or held as of right from original and immemorial possession, or from conquest in war waged between acknowledged sovereign parties to the war, intended never to divest themselves of it voluntarily.

The Spanish people, acting in their character of *one* supreme sovereignty and one people, intended, after defining the boundaries of and *creating* the proposed new states, to confer on them, to "*delegate*" to them the right to exercise as many of the "powers" of sovereignty as would answer the objects and purposes of local government. While those states would be politically independent of *each other* in relation to their own separate local affairs, would they be each an independent sovereignty of original, inherent and underived powers, looking to no source outside of itself for the warrant of those powers?

The statement of the question, after remembering what precedes it, carries its answer on its face; and that answer is, No, emphatically, No! Their status would be, as to the independent sovereignty question, precisely the same as was the status of the American Colonies of Great Britian before the breaking out of the Revolutionary war. The Colonies were totally independent of each otber, but they were all *dependent*, for the right which they enjoyed of exercising certain powers of sovereignty, on their great common sovereign, the King of Great Britain, who, in their respective charters, had "delegated" those powers to them, taking care at the same time to expressly reserve to himself as their liege sovereign the allegiance of the Colonies to himself the sovereign of the entire kingdom.

Now in this actual case of the Colonies, and in the supposed case of the confederation of the Spanish Provinces, the grantor of the right to exercise sovereign powers was and would be *exactly the opposite* of the granting parties in the case of the American Union. In the latter case the delegation of powers came *from the States* as the original sovereigns in the case existing prior to the Union, and *creating* a governmental machinery for that Union dependent *on them* for its origin and existence; whereas in the case of the Colonies, *they* were created by Great Britain, who delegated to them whatever powers they possessed; and in like manner, had the Spanish Confederation taken place, the creation of the Spanish States and the conferring of powers on them would have proceeded from that *one*, actually existing and sovereign community, "The People of Spain." Hence after the formation of the confederation, should the people of any one or more of these States, pleading the orders of their respective States, attempt to carry out an act of secession from the confederacy, they would plead authority which had never been conferred on those States by their still existing creator, and therefore, in obeying such unauthoritative orders, would rightfully become amenable as traitors and rebels to their real and only sovereign, "The People of Spain."

Through the voice of John Quincy Adams, her son and representative in Congress in 1836, Massachusetts again and for the thirteenth time proclaimed in that year her fealty to the doctrine of State Sovereignty. Mr Adams then, in the debate relative to the admission of Arkansas into the Union, termed Congress "the representative of that *federation* compounded partly of slave-holding and partly of entirely free States." The deduction from this utterance is of course that if the union of the States is *a federation*, then the parties to it, viz: the States, must necessarily be each an independent sovereign; for no political power outside of them claimed allegiance from or control of them.

For the fourteenth time, through the voice of this her great and gifted son, did Massachusetts, in 1839, repeat her belief in the great principle which she had for so many years upheld. Mr. Adams, in his oration delivered in that year on the jubilee of the Constitution, plainly countenanced the right of secession if, in the conscience of the people intending it, they should feel themselves to have grave and just causes for their action. In this oration he said, "to the people alone is thus reserved the *dissolving* as well as the constituent power, and that power can be exercised by them only under the tie of conscience binding them to the retributive justice of heaven. With these qualifications *we may admit* the same rights vested in the people of *every State* in the Union *with reference* to the General Government." Here, take notice, he concedes the right of *any* State to secede for cause; for he speaks of the States *disjunctively.*

Did the late Confederate States in their attempt at secession have justifying cause? Before answering this question, I must beg you as a reader of history to remember *that well known fact*, undisputed in any quarter, that the Union never would have been formed had not the stipulation for the surrender of fugitive slaves and the farther stipulation that any State might import slaves into her territory from abroad for twenty years, been inserted in the Constitution. To name nothing else, (but much more might be adduced,) let the great grievance, the deliberate, *avowed and long continued* infraction of the compact about to be specified, stand forth to the world, as it certainly does and did to the late Confederate States, as ample and justifying cause for their course in 1861. Remember that the abstract question of human freedom either in a state of nature or in organized civil society, the right or wrong of domestic slavery, could have nothing to do with the matter, as between the parties to the compact, *after* the compact *was signed.* The Northern States had signed the compact *with their eyes open*, and therefore *their* mouths, (whatever other and outside nations might justifiably or otherwise say or think of slavery,) were, by the rigid requirements both of good morals and religion, or ought to have been shut.

If I, as a private individual, voluntarily enter into a compact with even a notorious thief and utter scoundrel, in the provisions of which compact are some morally good and legal stipulations, but also others requiring me to act in collusion with him in the violation of good morals and law, all jurists and ethical writers as well as the plain dictates of common sense will tell me that I cannot rightfully hold him to *any* of his stipulations if I knowingly and deliberately infract one single stipulation myself—and that my voluntary agreement to the *whole* compact binds me to perform *every* part of it, if I would hold him to *any* part; and *vice versa*. If, at any time, after having entered into the bargain, my awakened conscience pricks my peace of mind, all that I, in the eye of good faith and good morals can do, is to retire from the *whole* thing, and of course leave *him* equal freedom, unless *he*, uncoerced and of his own free will, agrees to eliminate from the compact the part or parts I object to.

As a reader of history you must also remember that Massachusetts, as well as other Northern States, soon after acceding to the Union of 1789, passed a law to carry out in good faith that stipulation in the Federal Constitution which provided for the rendition of fugitive slaves. Fowler says, "The Legislature of Massachusetts, in aid of that provision of the Constitution intended to secure the restoration of fugitive slaves from their masters, passed a law by which negroes were prohibited, under the penalty of confinement, hard labour in the house of correction, and whipping not exceeding ten stripes, *from taking up their residence in the State.* Thus Massachusetts asserted her own State rights, and recognized the rights of the Slave-holding States."

We now come to that one justifying cause (out of many) before alluded to, for the secession of the Confederate States in 1861; and that is *the deliberate, persistent, and avowed nullification of the laws of Congress*, in relation to the rendition of fugitive slaves, by eleven of the Northen States after 1850, and thereby the gross violation by these eleven States of their solemnly pledged faith to fulfill that provision of the Constitution which stipulates for such rendition. In despite of the Constitution and the laws of Congress, and of the remonstrances of Virginia and other Southern States, these Northern nullifying States kept for many years the objectionable laws upon their statute books until the secession in 1861 of the Southern States. The names of the eleven States referred to are Maine, Massachusetts, Pennsylvania, Wisconsin, Vermont, New York, Michigan, Connecticutt, New Hampshire, New Jersey, and Rhode Island. [*See Report of the Committee of the Legislature of Virginia in* 1860.] And in relation to such action, and more similar to it, on the part of the Northern States, what did another great son of Massachusetts, Daniel Webster, (boasted of by the entire North as *the great expounder* of the Constitution,) say in his speech at Capon Springs, in 1851? Why this, "I do not hesitate to say and repeat, that if the Northern States refuse wilfully and deliberately to carry into effect that part of the Constitution which respects the restoration of fugitive slaves, *the South would no longer be bound to keep the compact.* A bargain broken on one side, *is broken on all sides!*" in other words, the Northern States, by their Personal Liberty bills, ("wilfully and deliberately" persisted in,) had virtually abrogated and abolished the Constitution! and as their only connection with the Southern States existed by and through the Constitution, *the compact*, hence, when that catastrophe took place, they had no more claim for political connection with the slave States than Russia or China had; and therefore no cause whatever for war against those States because the latter proposed and endeavoured to set up a separate confederacy for themseles without lifting or threatening to lift a finger against the Northern States; which latter act they would have been fully justified in doing, had they chosen to initiate the war, by that great feature or rule of the Laws of Nations, the *Lex Talionis*..

To show the spiteful animus of Massachusetts and her deliberate determination to execute her nullification law as to the rendition of fugitive slaves, it is only necessary to cite certain action on her part in 1857. In that year she ignominiously turned out of the office of Judge of her own Probate Court, Edward G. Loring, a U. S. Commissioner and a citizen of Massachusetts, because he refused to obey her own nullification law.—[*Fowler.*] Now if she did not consider herself a complete and independent sovereignty of original and inherent powers and a member only of a mere Confederacy of equals having no supreme ruler over them, how could she pretend to justify for her enactment of the law in question and the enforcement of one of its provisions in the case of Judge Loring?

But we have another and the fifteenth assertion by her of the doctrine of State Sovereignty, when, referring in April, 1856, to the provisions of the Federal Constitution relative to the powers granted to the United States respecting the writ of Habeas Corpus and the great right of the Trial by Jury, she made the following utterance through Governor Briggs, then a member of the House, and Chairman of the Committee reporting to the Legislature. "It was not that the States *relinquished* these rights to the keeping and protection of the Federal Government, * * * *. It was *a mutual agreement* among the *States*, to prevent *any* State so disposed from abrogating the cardinal principles of a free government by depriving the citizens of those rights." And he added, "with his excellency, [Governor Gardiner of Mass.] we believe that of the State rights retained by *each sovereign* member of the *confederacy*, the two cardinal ones are the habeas corpus and the trial by jury." And in the Committee's report he further added as follows: "State *sovereignty* on all subjects and in all things where the exercise of that sovereignty" [*mark*, he does not say the sovereignty of the *one* "People of the United States," but of the *States*,] has not been *delegated* to the United States, is *the language of* the *Constitution* and the safety of the *States*. This principle has *always* been regarded as vital to the existence and perpetuity of the States, a distinct and *independent power*. It was so claimed by *the fathers and founders of our institutions*." The Committee was reporting on the propriety or expediency of repealing Massachusetts' law nullifying that provision of the Constitution and those laws of the United States which required the surrender of fugitive slaves. Although the highest judicial authority in the State had declared this nullification law to be unconstitutional, yet the Committee, solely on the ground of the *independent sovereignty* of the State, recommended the retention of this nullification law on the statute book.

If the State was a mere political or municipal department of, and deriving its powers from, that imaginary sovereignty, that myth, "We the People of the United States," as asserted and contended for by Motley, then the Committee had not a shred of ground to stand on in their recommendation, but in this recommendation were simply traitors themselves inciting the members of the Legislature to commit treason. Here we have an important Committee of the Legislature of Massachusetts preaching the most ultra, Jeffersonian, South Carolina, State Rights and State Sovereignty doctrine that it was possible for them to do. The Committee say, and that too in strict accordance with the well known facts of the case, (relating not only to the writ of Habeas Corpus and Trial by Jury, but to *all* the provisions of the Constitution,) that those two great rights were stipulated for and secured, [Sect. 9, Article I, and Sect. 2d, Article III.] under a "*mutual agreement*," (therefore *a Treaty*,) between "the *States*," whereby each of the great contracting parties engaged itself to all the others and they to each that the two rights referred to should be secured to all the citizens of the *several* States. And why was this done? Why should Massachusetts or Connecticutt concern themselves about the rights and privileges of citizens of Virginia *within* Virginia, and be so very particular in requiring Virginia to promise the preservation of the privileges of these two cardinal rights to her own citizens within her own borders, over whom neither Massachusetts or Connecticutt could have any pretense of jurisdiction or rights of any kind within Virginia? Most plainly because of that other provision of the Federal compact, (the great Treaty between the States,) viz: Sect. 2d, Article IV, which says, "The citizens of each State shall be entitled to all privileges and immunities of citizens in the several States;" for otherwise, a citizen of Massachusetts or Connecticutt, if apprehended and indicted in Virginia, for an infraction of the laws of Virginia, might possibly be tried and condemned to imprisonment or death without having had the benefits of those two great securities of human rights and freedom.

If, as Massachusetts has authoritatively declared, Sec. 9, of Article I, and Sect. 2d, of Article III were not ordained by any *one* political community termed "We the People of the United States," then she declares, *ipsissima voce*, that not a single one of the provisions of the Federal Constitution was ordained and established by that political myth, "We the People of the United States;" for, surely it is hardly necessary to enter here into any argument to prove to any man of ordinary intelligence that whatever party or parties ordained any one Section or Article of the Federal Constitution ordained every word of it.

It may seem superfluous, after what has been said, to add the two items bearing on this point which now follow; but as they may be new and of some interest to some of the readers of this letter I will now do so.

To *very few* of the printed copies of the Constitution is appended its concluding declaration, which occurs immediately prior to the signatures of the delegates who framed it. It is in these words: "Done in Convention, by the unanimous consent of the *States* present, the 17th day of September," &c., &c. This declaration conclusively shows that the representatives of no *one* people framed the Constitution. The other item is this:

In January, 1830, in the celebrated debate in Congress on Foote's resolution, that eminent jurist, legislator and statesman, Edward Livingston, (afterward Secretary of State under President Jackson and a strong unionist,) said, "I place little reliance on the argument which has been *most depended on* to show that this is a popular government: I mean the preamble which begins with the words "we the people," It proves nothing more than the fact that the *people* of the *several* states" [that is, the *highest* power known in the state, instead of the Legislature,] "had been consulted and had given their consent to the instrument. To give these words any other construction would be to make them an assertion *directly contrary to the fact.* We know, and it has never been imagined or asserted," [he meant of course by intelligent and *honest* men, for he had just before referred to the words as having been used as an argument "most depended on,"] "that the People of the United States collectively *as a whole people* gave their consent, or were [even] consulted in that capacity."

Had Mr. Livingston chosen to do so, he could have given *from the record* the very interesting history of the preamble, (known now to but comparatively few people,) showing *how* the enumeration of the several states *by name*, (at first placed in it and voted for *unanimously*,) had, from a very peculiar and unexpected necessity of the case, arising in the later days of the Convention, been compelled to be eliminated from it in the last week of the four months' session, with the *very clearest and most explicit* understanding among *all* the framers that the *original* sense or meaning of the preamble, as indicated by the enumeration of the States by their names, was not to be in the slightest degree altered by this necessary elimination, and adoption of the present phraseology in the beginning of the preamble. He could have shown that so long as the enumeration of the States by name stood in the preamble, (viz: the entire period of the Convention except the last week,) the terminating words *now* in it, viz: that the Constitution was ordained "for the United *States* of America" *were not there;* and that when the enumeration was from necessity left out, *then*, and not before, were the words "for the United *States*" appended; showing plainly that these words were added as a substitute for and *an equivalent to the enumeration*, and to indicate that the Constitution was made not for *one* people but for the several "*States*." I can readily perceive why Mr. Livingston did not enter into the history referred to. He knew that he was addressing educated, intelligent statesmen well acquainted with the history of the Constitution, and that therefore a statement of the *details* of the history to them would be unnecessary. He consequently confined himself to giving only, in a few words, the inevitable deduction from that history.

Omitting here the details of the proceedings of the Legislature of Massachusetts in May, 1856, when in a joint resolution she does not ask, but imperiously "*demands*" [that is the word she uses,] of Congress in "her character as a *Sovereign State*" [what more could Great Britain call herself?] the institution of certain proceedings respecting the Brooks–Sumner affair; we will now take a hasty glance at some of her State Sovereignty utterances in 1855, '57 and '58.

In 1855 her Legislature passed the following resolution in relation to the Kansas troubles:

"This Commonwealth is ready if necessary to aid with *her whole power* the Governor of Kansas and the people of that Territory or of *any other territory or state* in support of Constitutional rights, by *whomsoever* infringed;"—the Commonwealth of course, from the very necessity of the case here presented, *to be the judge* as to what rights are constitutional or otherwise. It was well known at the time that, by the word "whomsoever," she specially referred to the Government of the United States. If then Massachusetts, (herself being the judge of the grievances of Kansas,) could rightfully use her entire military force or any portion thereof to right the grievances of that Territory, (not her own, mark you,) against *any* power or authority, how, in the name of consistency and common sense, could she condemn South Carolina for taking measures in 1832 to protect *herself* only (not outsiders,) from the effects of what that State judged, for herself, to be certain unconstitutional acts of Congress? Contrasting Massachusetts and South Carolina in this aspect of State action, we may with propriety say that while Massachusetts proposed to conduct the nullification business on a very extended wholesale scale, South Carolina could be regarded only as aiming at a mere petty retail operation in that line.

In connection with this very Kansas business, Mr. Wells, a leading member of the Legislature of Massachusetts, and acting with a majority of the House, said, in a speech on the Kansas resolution, "The sovereignty of Massachusetts *is older* than that of the Union, and *was not conferred by the Union.* [Very true.] The Declaration of Independence *is an avowal of State Rights.* [True again.] * * * * *. The powers of the United States are all granted by the *several States.*" [True to the letter.] In all this he was of course perfectly correct, for there stand the *facts* on the *record*, which, (to the Massachusetts of 1861 and of to-day,) like the "damn'd spot" on Lady McBeth's hand, will not "out" at her bidding.

Mr. Upham, in the Senate of Massachusetts, said in a speech on 7th May, 1857, "The American Union, as a body politic, consists *exclusively* of States *separate* and States *confederated.* Whatever does not belong to a *State*, as *one of the constituent* parts of the system, is not properly embraced by or in accordance with the true theory of our Government." In the first of above sentences he indicates in as few words as the thing can possibly be expressed or that I ever saw it done, the fact of the total independence (of the States) of each other as to their own internal affairs, and that, as to affairs in common between them under the compact, their dependence on or connection with each other is that only of a mere *confederation*, and therefore that the several people of the several States do not in any sense compose a political community of *one* people. In the second sentence he asserts the truth that *nothing* can belong to or be of the Union except as through the relationship to the Union *of the State* to which that thing belongs; and thus he explodes the idea that there can be any such political thing as *one* "People of the United States," outside of and distinct from their status as the several, separate, political bodies of people divided among and belonging to the several States. In his first sentence he also scouts the idea of there being *one* "People of the United States," in a political sense, by the use of the word "exclusively" in the connection in which it is found. Of course under such a Union as Mr. Upham describes, and as Massachusetts in her sovereign character as a State has often officially asserted it to be, the General Government can be nothing more than the mere agent of the sovereign parties to the compact; and in accordance with this truth, Franklin Pierce, (a New England man,) when President of the United States, termed the Government in one of his messages the "*general agent*" of the States.

Rufus Choate, a Massachusetts statesman of eminent ability, and often honored in his own State by its electing him to high office, said, (in his 4th of July address, in 1858.) of the States, that while they exist like "primordial particles of matter *indestructible* and *impenetrable*, whose natural condition is to *repel* each other, or at best to exist in their own *independent* identity, the Union is an *artificial* aggregation," [not a merger,] "of such particles." He continued, "have you ever considered that it was a *federative* system that we had to adopt? * * * * * *. There the states were when we became a nation. There they had been for one hundred and fifty years, for one hundred and seventy years. * * *. In the scheme of every statesman they remained a *component* part, unannihilated, *indestructible*. In the theories of all publicists and all speculators they were retained, and they were valued for it to hinder and disarm that *centralization* which had been found to be the *danger* and the *weakness* of federal liberty."

The Supreme Court of the United States has declared that the States sustain towards each other "*international*" relations.—[*Fowler*.] If so, the compact called the Constitution of the United States is a Treaty, a Governmental Treaty* embracing treaty stipulations as to inter-state and foreign commerce; as to rendition of fugitive slaves; as to fugitives from justice; as to traitors escaping from any state in which they had committed treason against such state; treaty stipulations as to laying and collecting taxes, duties &c., for the common purposes of the States confederated; also as to declaring war and making peace *in the name* of the *States*; and, in short, as to all the objects and purposes specified in the compact.

---

*As, in fact, are the constitutions of all confederacies to which the parties are sovereign, independent and politically equal States, confederating of their own free will and choice, and delegating powers to their General Government,

Did it ever specially strike you that in the enacting clause of all the laws of the United States not one word in it says that the laws are enacted in the name of, or by the representatives of the "*People* of the United States," but by the Senate and Representatives of the "States"? Yet in many of the States you will find that the enacting clause of their State laws says the laws are enacted in the name of, or by the representatives of, "*The People*" of the State. And why so? Because the people in each State are a political entity and are indeed the supreme sovereign power over the State, the fountain and origin of all the acts of the State. *Their* enacting clauses do not say "Be it enacted by the *Counties* of Massachusetts," &c., or "by the representatives of the Counties of Massachusetts;" for Massachusetts was not brought into existence by the fiat of her Counties. It was because of her *first* being Massachusetts, that *they* came into existence, and had their metes and bounds and powers set and defined by *her* fiat.

In her own State Constitution of 1820, which is I think her present Constitution, Massachusetts proclaims to the world her ancient political creed, that there is politically no such thing as "The People of the United States," and that she herself is a sovereign and independent State. Here is the passage:

"The people of this Commonwealth have the *sole and exclusive* right of governing themselves as a *free, sovereign and independent* State; and do and forever hereafter shall exercise and enjoy every power, jurisdiction and right which is not, or may not hereafter be, by them *delegated* to the United States of America in Congress assembled." Observe particularly that in this last clause nothing is said about *one* people being assembled (by their representatives) in Congress, but "*States* assembled in Congress" and that nothing is by her surrendered up and forever alienated to that supposed one people, but that whatever is granted by her is only "delegated" to the "*States*" when assembled in Congress.

I have in these pages given only a portion of the record of Massachusetts on State Sovereignty; but this portion is enough and more than enough to sustain me in saying that if she was right in the position taken according to that record and held by her for so long a period of time as it shows, then when in 1861 and subsequently she voted men and money to oppress, slaughter and subjugate the people of her sister states at the South, she thus voted and acted (on the testimony of *her own record,*) simply to perpetrate murder, arson and rapine on an innocent people who had given her, (by her own prior admissions,) even as a member of the Union, no provocation or pretext whatever for those horrible crimes against right, justice and humanity.

I could produce a similar record of her Northern sisters in iniquity, but as the maxim, "*ex uno omnes disce*," applies to those other States on the very best of foundations, viz: facts, it thus will render the labour unnecessary.

Before closing I will cite another *Northern* witness to the truth of the independent soveriegnty of the States. William Rawle, a Northern man, one of the most eminent jurists and publicists of his day, a high-toned Federalist, selected and appointed by Washington to be U. S. Attorney throughout his entire administration of eight years, and continued in the same office throughout the administration of John Adams, published in 1826, an elementary work on the Constitution. It has been generally regarded as the most accurate and able exposition of the Constitution. Emanating from a Federalist of the old Hamiltonian school, it was not to be thought possible that any treason could lurk in it. On account of its high reputation and intrinsic merit, it was adopted as the text-book at the U. S. Military Academy at West Point. There Lee, Davis, Johnston, Magruder, Huger, Pendleton, Beaureguard, Jackson and others of the Confederate Captains were taught, under the sanction and authority of the U. S. Government, the true principles of the Constitution. The principles thus and there instilled into their minds were couched in the following words of Rawle:

At page 302 Mr. Rawle says, "The secession of a State from the Union depends entirely *on the will of the people* of such State. * * *. In any manner by which a secession may take place, nothing is more certain than that the act should be deliberate, clear and unequivocal."

At page 287 Mr. Rawle says, "The States may wholly withdraw from the Union, but while they continue they must retain the character of representative republics."

In chapter 32, page 297, Mr. Rawle says, "If a faction should attempt to subvert the government of a State for the purpose of destroying its republican form, the paternal power of the Union could be called forth to subdue it. Yet it is not to be understood that its interposition would be justifiable if *the people* of a State should *determine to retire from the Union*, whether they adopted another or retained the same form of government." These were the doctrines taught *by the U. S. Government* to Lee, Davis, Beaureguard and others after them at West Point up to 1861.

And yet, when those Southern heroes, in strict accordance with the doctrines which, *under the sanction of the General Government*, had been instilled into their minds, retired from the service of the confederacy and (obeying each the call of his own sole sovereign, the State to which he belonged,) rallied to her defense in the armies of the new confederacy of her choice, they were, forsooth, traitors!

Traitors to what or to whom?

How came any of them to owe obedience, (not allegiance) to the laws of the confederacy known as the United States? Manifestly because of the fiat of his sovereign, *his own State*, directing him to pay such obedience when she acceded to the compact. Her act of accession was an order to him to obey the laws of the confederacy; her act of secession a release from such injunction. In one contingency only could he commit treason against a confederacy of which his own sovereign was a member, viz: when without the orders or sanction of that sovereign, he should rise up against the authority and oppose the laws of the Confederacy; and even in that case his acts would be treasonable only for the reason that in opposing those laws and resisting that authority, he would be opposing *his own Sovereign*, in her character as one of the makers of those laws, and as a constituent member of the partnership from which that authority emanated, and on which it was based.

As a well known axiom of political ethics, Independent, Sovereign States, whether members of a confederacy or not, can not by any possible act commit treason against any authority whatever. Hence it is that the treason clause in the Federal Constitution is applicable only and was intended to apply only to individuals. And hence it was that Seward and his unscrupulous confreres, (I say "Seward," for Lincoln was only a mere nose of wax in the hands of those usurpers,) knowing that Sovereign States, whether in or out of a Confederacy, are still existent States, whatever thay may do, (short of voluntary merger of their own nationality into that of some other nation,) affected to believe that the seceding States had committed political suicide by their acts of secession, (an utter impossibility, and Seward well knew it,) and so converted their citizens into a mob of insurrectionary individuals acting without any public authority and on their own separate, individual responsibility only.

Seward knew that the states adhering to the Union had the right under public law, (international law, or custom,) but not *as* the United States of *the Constitution*, to declare war against the Confederate States as Independent, Sovereign States for any cause that in their own opinion might seem just; and if they should choose to do so, to make the acts of secession this cause on the assigned ground (if they chose) of certain injury done to them the adhering states by such acts, and by assigning also in their list of grievances, (of course without any truth,) that such acts had no provocation whatever from the adhering states.

But Seward *dared not* take this position however much he may have wished to do so; for had he done so, he would have thereby *recognized the nationality* of the seceding States and their acts of secession as nationally authoritative acts, and he well knew the consequences of such a proceeding; viz: that the powers of Europe would have at once recognized the Seceding States and would thereby have given no cause of complaint to the adhering States; and that, from such recognition by the powers of Europe, certain other consequences would have inevitably followed, which would have rendered the subjugation of the seceding States an utter impossibility. Hence his affectation of believing the seceding States had committed that impossible thing, political suicide by their acts of secession.

Had Seward made war on the seceding States as still existent and recognized States, and, had admitted that they were actually out of the Union, and had he after this subjugated them, then there would have stood in his way no constitutional barriers, (the breaking through of which is yet to bring dire woe* to the Northern States,) against what, on Seward's theory, has been and is the utterly unjustifiable and unauthorized course which the General Government has taken (during and since the war,) towards the seceding States.

It is well known that Northern orators (in Congress and elsewhere,) and Northern newspapers of ability have often boasted of the unheard of magnanimity exhibited by the General Government in refraining, after

---

*The great historian, Froude, in a lecture recently delivered in New York, said.

"In my reading of history *one tremendous phenomenon* forever forces itself on my observation, viz: that every political crime is a debt registered in Heaven: and the payment *to the very last farthing, with interest and compound interest*, is demanded of those who, when the bill" [*compact*?] "is signed, represented the person of the criminal."

Massachusetts at least, cannot charge that the Southern States incurred any debt of the above nature when they seceded in 1861, nor aver that they paid for it by their sufferings and losses during and since the late war. Time will yet reveal who "represented the person of the criminal when the bill, [the compact] was signed."

In the same paragraph and in continuance of the same subject Froude says, "It was not those, [viz: the indentical individuals,] who committed the crime, who generally suffered for it" as observed by him in the teachings of history, *but those who came after them*; and as to this fact he adds, "this has been, from the beginning of time, one of the mysteries of the providential government of the world." If then political crime was committed by one or the other of the parties to the late war, the punishment *is yet to come*, according to the general operation of the phenomenon as observed by Froude.

the war ended, from bringing to trial, convicting and executing a single traitor (so-called) engaged in the late war. That men of general intelligence and erudition in public or international law, and well grounded in the history and provisions of the Constitution of 1789, should have the doubly brazen effrontery to talk about magnanimity to traitors, when speaking in reference to citizens of the late Confederate States, would surpass belief, were it not for the well known fact, (charged on them by people of their own section,) that such men, leaders in the party now ruling the country, do not recognize the binding character of moral or religious restraint on their political actions or words. Do not these revolutionists know that among all English-speaking people, inheritors of the great rights of Magna Charta, no man can be held to be guilty of crime until he shall first have been, under the rules of law, convicted of the crime, and judicially pronounced to be guilty?

To lay a foundation for their boast, to vindicate their claim to the virtue of magnanimity, this horde of revolutionists owed it to themselves, to their cause, and to the world, to bring to trial and to convict of treason, (if they could,) some great leader of the people of the Confederate States. Had they, after a fair trial under the law, convicted such an one of treason and condemned him to the legal penalty of the crime; but, refraining from the infliction of the penalty, had thereupon pardoned and discharged him, then and not until then, could they, with any decency or propriety, have boasted of their magnanimity to the people of the South.

Magnanimity indeeed! Was it magnanimous to *torture*, in the barbarous spirit of the mediæval ages, for many long, weary months in the stone case-mates of Fortress Monroe, a physically feeble old man, whom, (*fearing* to bring to trial,) they at last discharged, virtually *sine die*, untried and unconvicted? The great mass of their party do not know it, but nevertheless there can be no doubt of the fact that such leading, influential and thoughtful men among them, possessing brains, as were deeply versed in the lore of the law and the truths of the Constitution, (men like their Chases, their Speeds, their Reverdy Johnsons and numerous others of similar calibre,) knew that to bring Jefferson Davis or any other aider and abettor of the Confederate States to trial for treason alleged to have been committed against the United States in the late war, was to obtain a judicial acquittal of the person charged with the crime; (or rather act, for no crime was committed;) and hence the advice which they doubtless gave and urged, (for Andrew Johnson hadn't the brains to comprehend the situation,) that Mr. Davis should be discharged from prison under bail for his appearance in court whenever called upon to appear.

They *never mean* to call him; they *dare not* do so; for they know in advance what the verdict, (if ever rendered,) must be, and that consequently it would be a condemnation *in their own courts* of the entire proceedings of the Federal Government with reference to the war, and to their course towards the Southern States from March, 1861, to the present day.

With this verdict before the country and the world, and to go down forever on the pages of history, (backed up by the utterly overwhelming arguments and luminous exposition of the Constitution which would have been put forth by that giant in the law, Charles O'Conor,) where then would be their claim of being in the right in the late war? where would be their ground (transparent pretext as it is, even now without the verdict,) for calling any citizen of the late Confederate States a rebel? Where would be their justification, (shallow as that is, even now,) for the seas of blood of their own people which they caused to be shed, and for the expenditure of the billions of that people's money which they poured out like water in their unholy efforts to subjugate, oppress, and humiliate an unoffending people?

Until they shall have, by due process of law, convicted of treason some prominent and leading aider and abettor of the late Confederate States, common decency ought to close their mouths when they feel inclined to boast of their magnanimity to the people of the South, and to use the terms "rebels and traitors" as applicable to the citizens of those States engaged in any mode in aiding those States to sever their connection, under the Constitution, with the Northern States.

Thus without going farther than so much of the record of Massachusetts as I have here presented, (for, if I were to go beyond it in an elaborate essay on the subject, I could so pile a dozen Pelions on Massachusett's Ossa, as to bring out the right of secession as clear as the noon-day sun in an unclouded sky,) I think that you or any unprejudiced reader of these pages, of whatever political opinions he may be, must admit that this record conclusively proves, (or at least ought so to prove to every citizen of Massachusetts,) that the right of secession did exist, and that it was no infraction of the Constitution, but a right independent of and outside of the Constitution, and inhering necessarily in every member of a political Confederacy constituted not by the fiat of any *one* sovereign, political community, but brought into existence only by the " mutual agreement " of independent, *Sovereign* States, already existing as such before the compact of union was entered into.

I remain, dear sir, with much respect,

Yours very truly,

A SON OF NORFOLK.

———o———

Since the foregoing was written, and now (December,) while passing through the press, the following extract from a late number of the N. O. Picayune may be very appropriately appended as germain to the subject discussed in the preceding pages.

———o———

IS THE DEMOCRATIC PARTY DEAD?

(*From the New Orleans Picayune.*)

* * * * * * * * *

Now, by the light of the experience in which we exist, all men can see the inevitable fate of every free Government abandoning the principles of the Democratic party. Men may change in upholding them. Men may abandon them and draw the sword to extinguish them; but they live in the breasts of the people as the true and only principles of liberty. Despotism and tyranny only concentrate a purer vitalily. The fiercer the despotism—the stronger the money oligarchy which holds them down—the higher in all probability will be the spirit which worships them. And it is for such reasons as these that THE WORLD can rightly affirm that the Democratic party is not dead. Its principles are undying—its adherents are millions—and whether the party which shall bring these principles again undefiled into the politics of the United States shall call itself Democratic or any other name, it must rise up to the restoration of the Government of the United States to a free Government, *or revolutionary darkness, the sure sequence of central despotism*, must spread over the land.

www.ingramcontent.com/pod-product-compliance
Lightning Source LLC
LaVergne TN
LVHW011137110826
845150LV00008B/2382

* 9 7 8 1 4 1 8 1 9 3 6 3 8 *